T0387405

SEE IT GROW!

See Bell Peppers Grow

by Kirsten Chang

BLASTOFF! READERS

BELLWETHER MEDIA • MINNEAPOLIS, MN

Blastoff! Readers are carefully developed by literacy experts to build reading stamina and move students toward fluency by combining standards-based content with developmentally appropriate text.

Level 1 provides the most support through repetition of high-frequency words, light text, predictable sentence patterns, and strong visual support.

Level 2 offers early readers a bit more challenge through varied sentences, increased text load, and text-supportive special features.

Level 3 advances early-fluent readers toward fluency through increased text load, less reliance on photos, advancing concepts, longer sentences, and more complex special features.

★ **Blastoff! Universe**

Reading Level

Grade K

Grades 1–3

Grade 4

This edition first published in 2024 by Bellwether Media, Inc.

No part of this publication may be reproduced in whole or in part without written permission of the publisher. For information regarding permission, write to Bellwether Media, Inc., Attention: Permissions Department, 6012 Blue Circle Drive, Minnetonka, MN 55343.

Library of Congress Cataloging-in-Publication Data

LC record for See Bell Peppers Grow available at: https://lccn.loc.gov/2023000635

Editor: Elizabeth Neuenfeldt   Designer: Brittany McIntosh

Printed in the United States of America, North Mankato, MN.

Table of Contents

Colorful Peppers   4

How Do They Grow?   6

Fully Grown   18

Glossary   22

To Learn More   23

Index   24

Colorful Peppers

Bell peppers are sweet to eat.
They are colorful.
They grow on leafy plants.

5

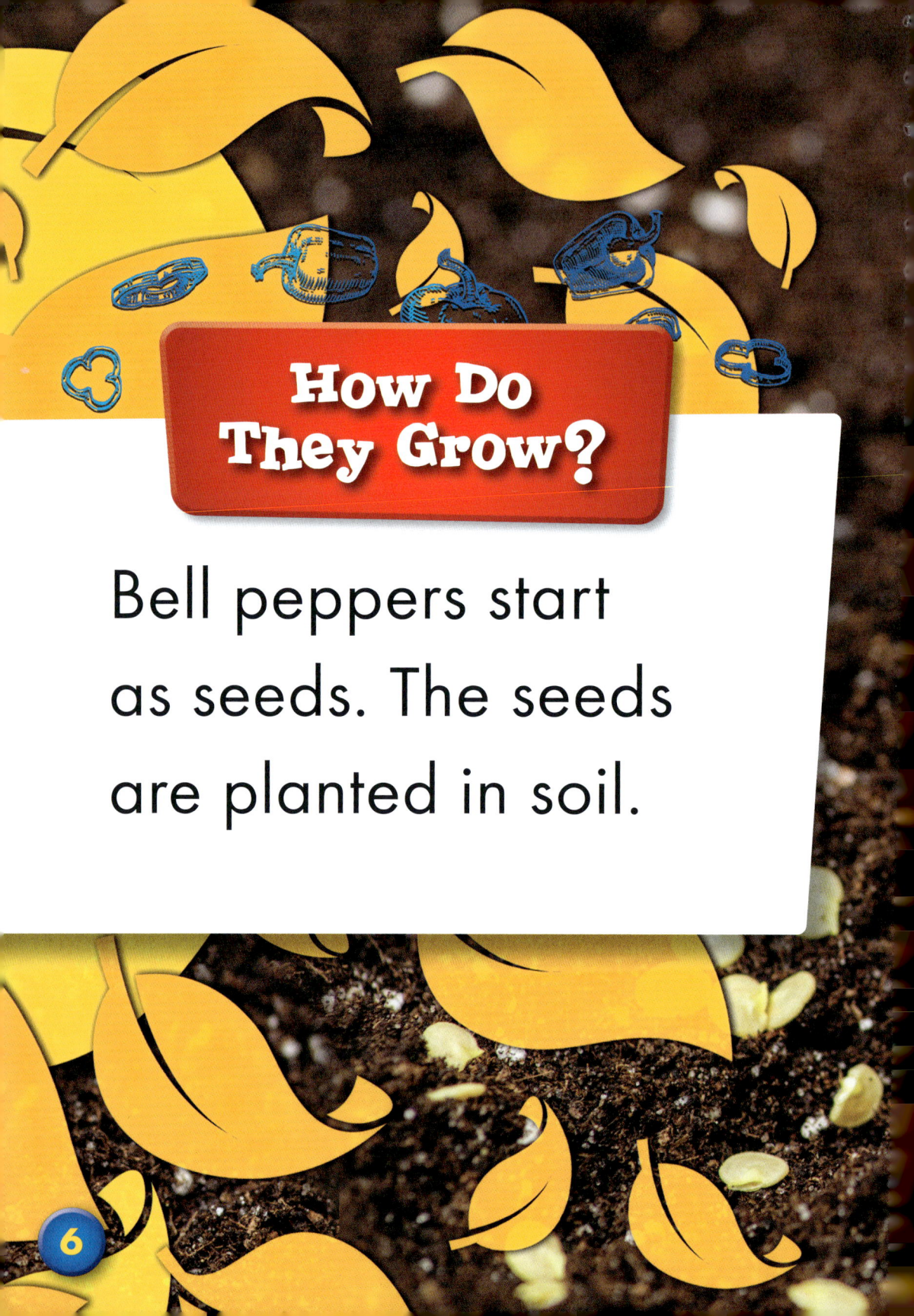

How Do They Grow?

Bell peppers start as seeds. The seeds are planted in soil.

seeds

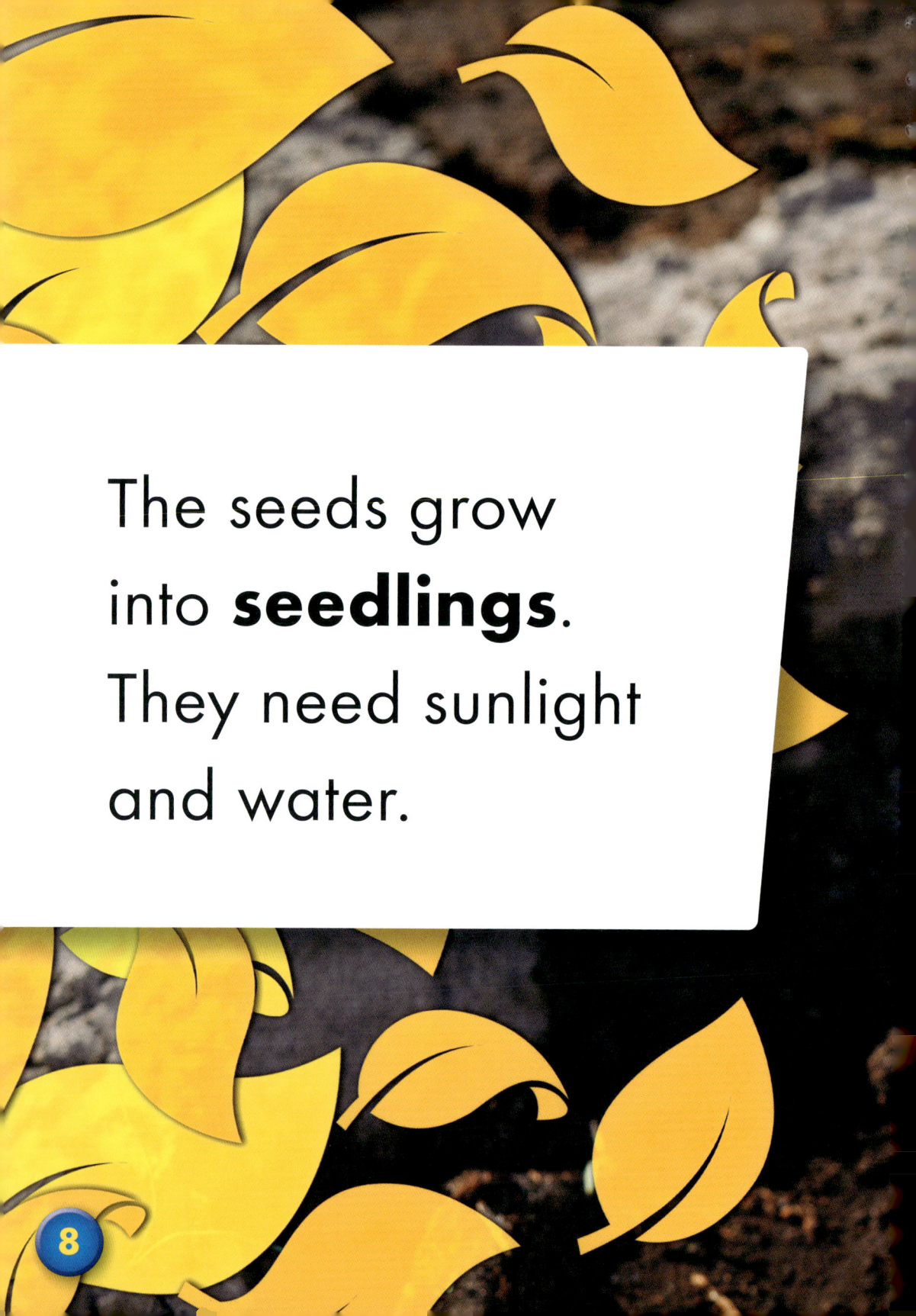

The seeds grow
into **seedlings**.
They need sunlight
and water.

Needed to Grow

soil

sunlight

water

seedling

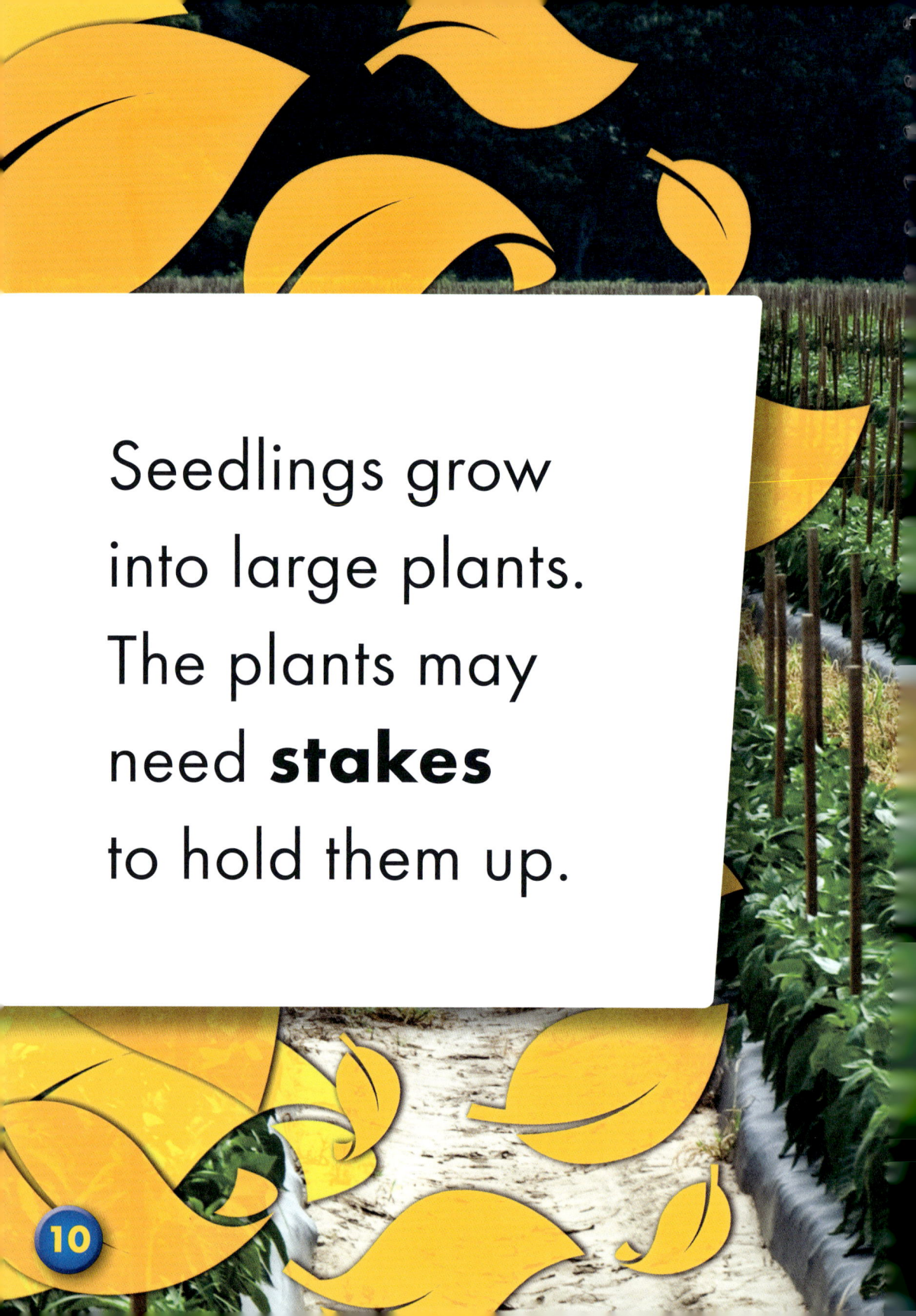

Seedlings grow into large plants. The plants may need **stakes** to hold them up.

10

stake

Flowers grow on the plants. Bees help **pollinate** the flowers.

flower

13

Peppers grow
from the flowers.
They start out green.

The peppers **ripen**.
They change color
to red, orange,
or yellow.

16

Fully Grown

Farmers cut the bell peppers from the plants. There are many seeds inside!

Bell Pepper Life Cycle

1  seeds are planted

2   plants grow

3   flowers bloom

4  bell peppers grow

We can eat
bell peppers
in many ways.
They are
a tasty treat!

Using Bell Peppers

stuffed peppers

salads

dipped in hummus

Glossary

pollinate

to move a dust called pollen to make seeds grow

stakes

pieces of wood that hold up plants

ripen

to become ready to eat

seedlings

small, young plants

To Learn More

AT THE LIBRARY

Chang, Kirsten. *See an Avocado Grow.*
Minneapolis, Minn.: Bellwether Media, 2024.

Jaycox, Jaclyn. *The Life Cycle.* North
Mankato, Minn.: Pebble, 2020.

Newland, Sonya. *Plants.* North Mankato,
Minn.: Capstone Press, 2020.

ON THE WEB

FACTSURFER

Factsurfer.com gives you
a safe, fun way to find
more information.

1. Go to www.factsurfer.com.

2. Enter "see bell peppers grow" into
   the search box and click 🔍.

3. Select your book cover to see a list of
   related content.

Index

bees, 12
colors, 4, 14, 16
cut, 18
eat, 4, 20
farmers, 18
flowers, 12, 13, 14
life cycle, 19
needed to grow, 9
plants, 4, 10,
  12, 18
pollinate, 12
ripen, 16
seedlings, 8, 9, 10
seeds, 6, 7, 8, 18
soil, 6

stakes, 10, 11
sunlight, 8
using bell peppers,
  21
water, 8